Kurt Vonnegut, Jr.'s

Slaughterhouse-Five

Text by
Tonnvane Wiswell
(M.A., Arizona State University)

Dr. M. Fogiel
Chief Editor

Illustrations by
Matteo DeCosmo

 Research & Education Association

MAXnotes® for
SLAUGHTERHOUSE-FIVE

Printed in the United States of America

Library of Congress Catalog Card Number 96-67404

International Standard Book Number 0-87891-045-X

MAXnotes® is a registered trademark of
Research & Education Association, Piscataway, New Jersey 08854

What **MAXnotes®** *Will Do for You*

This book is intended to help you absorb the essential contents and features of Kurt Vonnegut Jr.'s *Slaughterhouse-Five* and to help you gain a thorough understanding of the work. The book has been designed to do this more quickly and effectively than any other study guide.

For best results, this **MAXnotes** book should be used as a companion to the actual work, not instead of it. The interaction between the two will greatly benefit you.

To help you in your studies, this book presents the most up-to-date interpretations of every section of the actual work, followed by questions and fully explained answers that will enable you to analyze the material critically. The questions also will help you to test your understanding of the work and will prepare you for discussions and exams.

Meaningful illustrations are included to further enhance your understanding and enjoyment of the literary work. The illustrations are designed to place you into the mood and spirit of the work's settings.

The **MAXnotes** also include summaries, character lists, explanations of plot, and section-by-section analyses. A biography of the author and discussion of the work's historical context will help you put this literary piece into the proper perspective of what is taking place.

The use of this study guide will save you the hours of preparation time that would ordinarily be required to arrive at a complete grasp of this work of literature. You will be well prepared for classroom discussions, homework, and exams. The guidelines that are included for writing papers and reports on various topics will prepare you for any added work which may be assigned.

The **MAXnotes** will take your grades "to the max."

Dr. Max Fogiel
Program Director

Contents

> **Each Chapter includes List of Characters, Summary, Analysis, Study Questions and Answers, and Suggested Essay Topics.**

SECTION ONE

Introduction

The Life and Work of Kurt Vonnegut, Jr.

Kurt Vonnegut, Jr. was born on November 11, 1922 in Indianapolis, Indiana. His father was a prominent architect and his mother the daughter of a wealthy brewer. They were liberal, atheistic, and well-to-do third generation Germans who were prominent in the social scene of their city.

Although Vonnegut's older brother and sister were both educated in private schools, the Depression caused such a dramatic drop in the family income that the Vonneguts could no longer afford such luxuries as continuing to pay for Vonnegut's education. The change was traumatic for Vonnegut's parents and eventually led to his mother Edith's suicide in 1944. Vonnegut adjusted well to public school, where he started writing as a reporter for the newspaper at Shortridge High School.

Vonnegut enrolled in Cornell in 1941. At his father's recommendation that he study something practical, Vonnegut majored in chemistry. He continued to write, eventually becoming editor of the student paper at Cornell University.

In 1942, Vonnegut enlisted in the army. He was captured by Germans on December 22, 1944, after the Battle of the Bulge. From the front he was eventually sent to the open city of Dresden. While he was there, the Allies firebombed the city, killing 130,000 people. (By comparison, about half that number died in the bombing of Hiroshima.) Vonnegut survived only because his prison was a meat locker 60 feet underground.

After the war, Vonnegut married Jane Marie Cox, with whom he would have three children. He briefly attended the University of Chicago, then moved to Schenectady, New York, where he worked as a publicist for General Electric. During this time Vonnegut began to sell stories to such publications as *Collier's* and the *Saturday Evening Post.* Encouraged by his successes, he left his position at G.E. to pursue writing full-time in 1950.

Vonnegut's first full-length novel was *Player Piano*, published in 1951. His next novel, *Sirens of Titan*, was not published until 1959. Although this may have been the least successful part of his career, he did manage to support his family, including three nephews adopted when his sister died, from the earnings brought in by the short stories he wrote during this period.

Vonnegut's next book was *Mother Night* (1961), which was followed rapidly by *Cat's Cradle* (1963) and *God Bless You, Mr. Rosewater* (1965). Vonnegut turned to teaching in 1965, eventually coming to the University of Iowa's Writer's Workshop. While there, he was offered a three book contract, which was followed in short order by a Guggenheim fellowship. These fortuitous events led to the writing of *Slaughterhouse-Five*, which was published in 1969.

Slaughterhouse-Five was a success both critically and financially. Since its publication, Vonnegut has pursued writing full-time, producing eight more novels and many other works. His most recently published work is 1995's *Timequake*.

Historical Background

World War II started in September, 1939, when Germany invaded a heavily resisting Poland. France and Great Britain, which had signed an alliance with Poland, had been attempting to restrain Nazi aggression through diplomatic measures, but the invasion forced them to declare war. Meanwhile, the United States, which was in an isolationist mood carried over from World War I, declared itself neutral.

Because of its discipline, organization, and firepower, Germany was very successful and quickly overran the Poles. The Allies were able to do little against the German juggernaut, in great deal because of the outdated nature of their armies. While they had chosen to rest on their victor's laurels, the Germans had

aggressively modernized their army, devoting special resources to their air force. This led to the development of the dive bomber, which flew at low altitude to hit enemy targets, and aircrafts capable of flying for longer distances, permitting the bombing of targets far behind enemy lines.

These resources came to bear in the Battle of Great Britain (1940-1941), which was conducted almost entirely in the air. German forces bombed military targets, but Great Britain's extensive radar network limited their effectiveness, and there were few casualties. Not until Britain sent a force to bomb Berlin did Hitler aim the German aircraft at civilian targets in Britain. Fortunately, the Germans refused to launch a land-based invasion and turned their attention instead toward the U.S.S.R..

While the United States covertly aided the British throughout this period, it was not until the bombing of Pearl Harbor in December of 1941 that the United States officially entered the war. At this time, Great Britain was only hanging on, and France had long fallen. Britain, the United States, and the U.S.S.R. spent much time strategizing, deciding to pursue war on other fronts before tackling the Germans on the continent.

In early 1944, the Allies pursued a campaign of air warfare against the Germans that was designed not only to take out military and industrial targets but to sap the will of the people by attacking civilian sites. Incendiary bombing played a significant role in these raids, leading to a great loss of life. Then, in June of 1944, after the fall of Mussolini, the Allies invaded German-occupied France through Normandy. The quick Allied victories as the Nazis were routed from France came as a surprise, and the Allies did not pursue their advantage as well as they might have. However, as the German forces were pushed behind their own borders, they began to resist more strongly. By November, the two sides had come to a stalemate.

In this interim, the German forces regrouped. Hitler called for Total Mobilization, forcing every able bodied male between 16 and 60 into the army. These reserve forces allowed the Germans to surprise the Allied forces in the Battle of the Bulge, which took place in weakly defended Ardenne hills on December 14, 1944. Kurt Vonnegut was involved in this battle, which resulted in the death of 120,000 Germans and 75,000 Americans. It was the last great German offensive action.

In preparation for the invasion of Germany, the Allies intensified their aerial bombardment of Germany in early 1945. The culmination of these attacks was the levelling of refugee-swollen Dresden on February 13-14, 1945, an attack which was led by the British forces. While the Allies claimed Dresden was an important communication and transportation hub, there is now little doubt that its destruction served no military purpose, especially since the Dresden railyard was damaged so little that it was functioning again within three days. At a loss estimated at 130,000 civilian lives, most of whom died as a result of a firestorm that reached 1000 degrees Fahrenheit rather than the bombing itself, the casualties exceeded those of Hiroshima and Nagasaki. This is the overlooked tragedy that Vonnegut records in *Slaughterhouse-Five* .

Germany collapsed in the spring of 1945, as the Allies pushed in from the west and the Soviets from the east. After Hitler committed suicide, his successor surrendered on May 8, 1945, ending the war in Europe. In a few more months, Japan too surrendered, but the face of the world and of warfare would never be the same.

Kurt Vonnegut's wartime experiences provide the grist for the formative, and most relevant, life experiences of Billy Pilgrim. Vonnegut's participation in the war took place at a historical cusp. The Battle of the Bulge, in which he fought, was the only time the Germans had the kind of radical successes against American forces that would allow them to take prisoners. Hitler's last gasp, the Total Mobilization, is reflected in Billy/Vonnegut's description of the German soldiers who capture them, a motley group containing a poorly-shod and dressed teenager as well as two extremely old men.

The hostility of the Germans toward the Russians, who by the time of Billy/Vonnegut's capture had killed over a million German soldiers, is epitomized by Billy's eerie encounter with a starving, yet still very much human, Russian prisoner of war. Within the text, this episode contrasts strongly with the depiction of the British prisoners, who seem to benefit from the same positive attitude that kept Hitler seeking a British surrender instead of British annihilation. They are fit and healthy, while the Russians are dying from hunger and the cold. It would have been difficult for Vonnegut not to notice the difference even if he did not know the reason for it.

The developments in warfare also strongly affected Vonnegut's experience. The use of firebombing was only made possible by the invention of longer-range aircraft. The strategy of attacking civilian targets (ostensibly for "demoralization") was also quite novel. (As noted, the German forces themselves aimed only for military targets until the British initiated the practice against Berlin. German civilians suffered far more heavily as a result of this "tactic" than the British, who were protected by their coastal radar network.)

The Germans also had not prepared for firestorms resulting from incendiary bombing, as the effect had only been discovered a short time before in Hamburg. Without numerous deeply-dug bomb shelters, there was no way for such a large population to escape the killing effects of high heat and oxygen depletion. The development of long-range bombers, the decision to firebomb civilians, and the lack of an effective warning system or shelter were all responsible for the destruction of Dresden and the slaughter of its unsuspecting populace. Oddly, Vonnegut's meat locker prisoner, which would doubtlessly been repulsive to the Dresden populace, preserved him from the firestorm's effects.

It is worthwhile to note that the personalized narrative Vonnegut is able to provide this event is itself original, or at least it was at the time the book was published. After the end of World War II, the Dresden catastrophe was swept under the rug. Military histories avoided its mention and official information on the incident was classified long beyond any reasonable time. The only possible explanation for this "oversight" is the one cited at the end of *Slaughterhouse-Five* by a military hawk: the "true story" upsets anyone with a conscience. Even the British attempted to retreat from their "accomplishment," realizing that the bombing of a defenseless population of civilians inhabiting one of the most beautiful cities in Europe had almost no support among their own people.

For a long time the pretense was held that the city was of some military importance; but as *Slaughterhouse-Five* reminds the reader over and over, this simply was not true. And as David Irving documents in his seminal *The Destruction of Dresden*, the railyards were completely missed, while the historical center of the city was turned into a kiln that baked human beings into little bricks. The reason for the bombing seems to descend into a combination of gross callousness and the desire to get revenge on the Germans. Noteworthily, the raid on Dresden took place long before the concentration camps came to light.

Irving's book was also inspirational to Vonnegut, as it was the first fully-researched documentation of the attack on Dresden, its causes and its aftermath. It makes clear the innocent situation of the Dresdeners, who, although short on food, felt safe thanks to Dresden's status as an "open city." This same belief led the city's leaders to not consider heavy-duty bomb shelters a priority. Finally, the myth of Dresden's safety made is a magnet for refugees fleeing the Russian advance. Unfortunately, these mistakes resulted in even more deaths when the city was finally attacked.

Yet the *Destruction of Dresden* maintains a detached air, even in its descriptions of basements filled to wading depth with human gore and water tanks loaded with boiled corpses. Hiroshima was truly a tragedy, but few people know that more people died in the Dresden firestorm (and in fire-bombed Tokyo) than in the wake of the Enola-Gay. *Slaughterhouse-Five* is often the first time an American will ever have heard of these events. It was up to Vonnegut to bring this tragedy to the notice of the world in a way no one could forget, and in a way that could only ring so true with his own experiences behind it.

Vonnegut wrote *Slaughterhouse-Five* during the Vietnam war years. Protests against the war were numerous, but the feeling of inevitable victory ran high in many quarters. Simultaneous with the national debate over the war, the 1960s were marked by advances and setbacks in American race relations. The civil rights movement had had many successes, but there had also been rioting in some cities.

Before Vonnegut finished *Slaughterhouse-Five*, both Robert Kennedy, hero of the anti-war movement, and Martin Luther King would be dead. Their deaths started a loss of optimism in American life that would receive its *coup de grace* in the Seventies from Watergate and the miltary fiasco in Vietnam.

The 1960s were a pivotal era in the advancement of the fictional form. Black humor met with great success during this time. Most notable among its practitioners was Joseph Heller, author of *Catch-22*. Black humor acknowledged the absurdity of the world's workings, making this absurdity a matter for laughter. Man's inability to affect his fate was accepted as the status quo.

Vonnegut was categorized as a black humorist for some time, along with such outstanding authors as Terry Southern and John Barth. It was not a dishonorable characterization, but rather limiting to the critical analysis of his work. Much worse was his earlier label of science fiction author, a result of the futuristic setting of his first two novels, the dystopian *Player Piano* and the space opera parody *Sirens of Titan*. Such a description ignored his short story work and pigeonholed Vonnegut as a participant in a genre generally considered to have no literary value. This one-dimensional tag was likely the cause of Vonnegut's failure to be included on *Esquire*'s mid-fifties list of "every living American writer of even the slightest merit," an oversight which bothered him for years.

Despite the brilliance of his work of the early sixties (especially *Cat's Cradle*), the turgid prose of *Player Piano* and the fantastic setting of *Sirens of Titans* dogged Vonnegut's reputation into these years. However, among the reading public, his books were selling well enough during this time to merit their reprinting in 1966. He had became increasingly popular among college students, thanks in part to the word of mouth that had led to *Sirens of Titan* selling for fifty dollars a copy during the years it was out of print.

The first scholarly article to be published on Vonnegut finally appeared in 1966. But Vonnegut's battle to be taken seriously was far from over. Now, however, his popularity, which skyrocketed with the publication of *Slaughterhouse-Five*, and his vernacular style were used as weapons against him. One critic, Stanley Schatt, criticized his novels as "simplistic philosophy of kindness packaged in sophomoric tales that catered to the whims of unsophisticated readers." While his popularity enabled Vonnegut to devote himself once again to writing full time, critics still found it difficult to believe that a writer could appeal to the masses and still be good.

Despite the doubts of some contemporary critics, *Slaughterhouse-Five* was the work that sealed Vonnegut's reputation as one of the best authors of the modern age. Nineteen seventy-one became the banner year for academic criticism of Vonnegut, and 1972 saw the first book devoted entirely to Vonnegut's writings .

The analyses of Vonnegut's works have improved as he has aged. Recent titles have tackled such topics as the psychological states of his characters and the paradigm of Eden within his books. Yet, as late as 1989, Robert Merril, editor of *Critical Essays on Kurt Vonnegut,* asked for Vonnegut to be "taken more seriously by more critics.

The difficulty of this hinges on the fact of Vonnegut's continued output, which makes every analysis of his opus contingent on his next piece. Yet time will doubtlessly be kind to him, because his works are of lasting merit. One can only wish him to continue to keep critics of his works pleading contingency by continuing to write more of them.

Master List of Characters

Bernard V. O'Hare—*Vonnegut's fellow American prisoner of war and peacetime friend; He accompanies Vonnegut on his return back to Dresden.*

Mary O' Hare—*Bernard's pacifist wife; She accuses Vonnegut of planning to glamorize war.*

Billy Pilgrim—*The time-travelling protagonist; He primarily varies between being a chaplain's assistant taken prisoner of war by the Germans and between his later life as a successful optometrist.*

Barbara Pilgrim—*Billy's daughter; She is worried that her father has lost his mind.*

Tralfamadorians—*According to Billy, creatures from outer space who can see in the fourth dimension (time) and who kidnaps Billy.*

Roland Weary—*A cruel American soldier; He is thrown together with Billy and two scouts after the Battle of the Bulge.*

Billy's mom (no name given)—*A sad, quiet woman who tries to make meaning in her life out of things purchased in gift shops.*

Paul Lazzaro—*A rabid little American soldier who has sworn to make Billy Pilgrim pay for the death of Roland Weary's.*

Edgar Derby—*A middle-aged American school teacher who will be shot in Dresden for stealing a teapot; He is kind to Billy.*

Eliot Rosewater—*A patient next to in Billy in the mental ward; He introduces Billy to the works of Kilgore Trout.*

Valencia Merble—*Billy's fiancee, and later wife; She is overweight and materialistic.*

Montana Wildhack—*Star of stag movies and Billy's mate in the Tralfamadorian zoo.*

Howard W. Campbell, Jr.—*An American Nazi propagandist who tries to recruit American P.O.W.s into the "Free American Corps."*

Kilgore Trout—*A reclusive science fiction author; He becomes friends with Billy.*

Maggie White—*A beautiful, if simple woman married to one of Billy's fellow optometrists.*

Robert Pilgrim—*Billy's son, a Green Beret fighting in Vietnam.*

Bertram Copeland Rumfoord—*A history professor in the hospital with Billy; He refuses to believe Billy was in Dresden.*

Lily Rumfoord—*Rumfoord's trophy wife.*

Wild Bob—*A colonel whose regiment has been destroyed, causing his mind to snap. His rantings at the German railyard disturb Billy.*

Summary of the Novel

Chapter One is a preface-like chapter in the novel. Vonnegut describes the difficulty of writing *Slaughterhouse-Five*. Although he felt his war experiences needed to be written, he feels the finished product is a failure.

Billy Pilgrim travels in time. Most of his travels revolve around his experiences as a prisoner of war in World War II. Because he is a time traveller, he always knows what the outcome of each experience will be.

Billy, who was recently in a plane crash, is eager to tell the world about the wisdom of the planet Tralfamadore, whose residents kidnapped him. While his daughter berates him, he travels to his war experiences. After a major battle, Billy is hiding behind enemy lines with three other soldiers. One of them is Roland Weary, who is about to beat Billy, when they are captured by the Germans.

On his march to the railyards, Billy time travels to his optometry office in Ilium. He listens to a speech at the Lion's club in favor of blanket bombing in Vietnam, then goes home for a nap. He returns to World War Two. At the railyards, the prisoners are loaded onto boxcars for transportation to the prison camps.

Next Billy time travels to the moment when the Tralfamadorian spaceship kidnapped him, then returns to the boxcar. Roland Weary is dead when the prisoners arrive at the German prison camp. After a few days there, during which time Billy time travels to the mental ward where he stayed after the war, his death, the Tralfamadorian zoo, and his wedding night, the Americans are sent to Dresden.

The Americans are housed in an abandoned slaughteryard in Dresden. Billy relives the plane crash and his rescue. Back in Dresden, he and his friend, Edgar Derby, work at a malt syrup factory.

During an air raid, Billy travels to his seventeenth wedding anniversary party, where a barbershop quartet dredges up a suppressed memory of the bombing of Dresden. He then goes to the zoo on Tralfamadore, where he tells his beautiful mate, Montana, about his memory. After the flames of Dresden have died down, the prisoners and their guards leave the gutted city in search of food and shelter, finally staying at an inn outside of the city.

Billy's wife, Valencia, dies on her way to see him in the hospital after the plane accident. Because of his silence after the crash, he is considered a vegetable. He finally speaks to Bertram Rumfoord, telling him that he was in Dresden when it was bombed, and that the Tralfamadorians had taught him that the destruction of Dresden had to be. After being discharged, Billy sneaks off to New York and gets on a radio show, where he talks about the Tralfamadorians. Vonnegut says that he hopes Billy's philosophy is wrong.

Billy is put to work digging the corpses out of the rubble. Edgar Derby is shot for looting a teapot. One day, the war is finally over. Billy walks free into the springtime world.

Estimated Reading Time

Slaughterhouse-Five is a simply written and short book. It should take about seven hours to read the entire work. After doing so, it would be good for the student to reread the book to facilitate comprehension of Vonnegut's style.

SECTION TWO

Chapter 1

New Characters:

Kurt Vonnegut: *the author and occasional narrator*

Bernard V. O'Hare: *Vonnegut's fellow American prisoner of war*

Mary O' Hare: *Bernard's pacifist wife*

Summary

Vonnegut begins what is otherwise a work of fiction with some straightforward commentary from the author. Before the fiction begins in Chapter Two, Vonnegut announces that most of *Slaughterhouse-Five* is based in truth. He was a prisoner of war in Dresden near the end of World War II, and while he was there he witnessed its firebombing by the Allied Forces. He returned to Dresden in 1967, with his friend, Bernard O'Hare, in preparation for writing this book.

Vonnegut says that it has been very difficult for him to write about the destruction of Dresden. He worked on his Dresden book for years, coming back to it again and again. He was told that there was no purpose in his writing a book that would essentially be anti-war, since wars were about as inevitable as glaciers.

Vonnegut initially contacted his friend, Bernard O'Hare, to ask for help in remembering the war. O'Hare said he didn't remember much and was generally unenthusiastic. Vonnegut told him that he thought the climax of his book would be when Edgar Derby was shot for stealing a teapot, a situation which Vonnegut found tremendously ironic.

In his attempts to write this book, Vonnegut had attempted to outline its plot. His favorite outline was one done in crayon on the back of a roll of wallpaper. The end of this outline was the exchange of soldiers between the American and the Russian forces. At this point, O'Hare and Vonnegut, and the American who inspired the character Paul Lazarro, were all sent back to a rest camp in France before their return to the States.

Vonnegut then talks about his life after the war. He studied anthropology for a while at the University of Chicago, during which time he worked as a police reporter. In those days, neither Vonnegut nor most other Americans knew that the air raid on Dresden had been more destructive than the atomic bombing of Hiroshima. When Vonnegut described his planned book to a professor, the professor reminded Vonnegut of the German atrocities against the Jews. Vonnegut could only inadequately respond that he was aware.

Vonnegut then went to Schenectady, New York, where he worked in public relations for General Electric. Vonnegut describes this period in his life as the scrawny years. He and his wives were friends with many other veterans in Schenectady. Vonnegut notes that the kindest of the veterans they knew there were the ones who had really fought during World War II. These men were also the ones who truly hated war. Vonnegut attempted to do some research on Dresden while in Schenectady, but the Air Force refused to release the information he asked for on the grounds that it was secret.

Around 1964, Vonnegut finally went to visit Bernard O'Hare. Although they sat around for a while, they were unable to recall any good stories about the war. Meanwhile, Vonnegut was disconcerted by the unexplained hostility of Bernard's wife, Mary. Finally, Mary accused Vonnegut of planning to write a book which would glorify war, thereby promoting death. Vonnegut promised her he wouldn't, adding that he would call his book "The Children's Crusade."

Vonnegut went on to teach at the University of Iowa's Writers Workshop. During this time, he was given a contract to write three books. *Slaughterhouse-Five* is the first of these books. Vonnegut apologizes to the man who gave him the contract for the shortness and disorganization of his book. He explains that there simply isn't much intelligent to say about a massacre.

Vonnegut then remembers the night he spent in a hotel before he left for Dresden. He had two books with him: one, a book of poetry, and the other a biography of the French writer Celine. Vonnegut picks up the Gideon Bible and reads of the destruction of Sodom and Gomorrah. Even though Lot's wife was turned to a pillar of salt for looking back at the burning cities, Vonnegut loves her for being so human. He is no longer going to look back after finishing *Slaughterhouse-Five*.

He then tells the reader that his book is a failure. He ends the chapter by quoting the opening and closing lines of the fictional sections of *Slaughterhouse-Five*.

Analysis

In this preface-like first chapter, Vonnegut details the difficult process of writing about his war time experiences in Dresden. He does not say specifically what has caused him to have so much trouble writing his "Dresden book," but he does give many clues as to why almost a quarter of a century passed before he finally produced *Slaughterhouse-Five*.

First, Vonnegut's intent was not to glorify his experience. By choosing to write an anti-war book, he left himself with no strong models to follow. (Joseph Heller's infamous *Catch-22*, which also dealt with the randomness and misery of war, preceded *Slaughterhouse-Five* by a mere eight years.) As Mary O'Hare bitterly notes, war has generally been portrayed as a noble enterprise. Yet, like the other kind veterans Vonnegut met in Schenectady, Vonnegut knows this is not so. For this reason, his attempt to portray the events which he experienced would need to be written in a new style, one which Vonnegut himself created within this book.

Second, in dealing with the events surrounding the firebombing of Dresden, Vonnegut has to manage the ignorance he and most other people have on the topic. This ignorance was fostered by the United States military's decision not to release information on the bombing for a considerable time after the end of the war. While a lack of factual information may have delayed Vonnegut's production of his own account of this event, the general lack of public awareness provided Vonnegut with the opportunity to shock his audience in a way that could not be easily done with a better-known topic.

Yet underneath all of this must lie a deeper reason for Vonnegut's "Dresden book" paralysis. Although he does not mention it in the novel, during the time when he was supposedly working on his Dresden novel, he completed five other books and a plethora of short stories. What was it that kept driving him back to the event, like the man in the limerick Vonnegut quotes, yet kept his thoughts in an unproductive loop? Why didn't Vonnegut just turn his back to Dresden, like Lot and his daughters did at Sodom and Gomorrah?

Vonnegut's obsession indicates the indelibility of the horrors he witnessed in the aftermath of the bombing of Dresden. The images he will describe in the rest of the book with such dispassion were so upsetting that Vonnegut could not escape them. Such circularity and paralysis seem to indicate that he was suffering from post-traumatic stress syndrome. A less intelligent man might have snapped mentally; instead, Kurt Vonnegut produced one of the masterpieces of modern literature.

While it might have been easier for Vonnegut to attempt to block his memories, he attempted instead to cope with them through writing. The task must have been as onerous as Vonnegut describes it in this first chapter. His humanistic sensibilities would neither let him glorify the events which he lived through, nor allow him to justify them by dehumanizing the people who burned to death in Dresden as the evil enemy. Instead, he needed to convey the message that all war is tragic.

By doing so, Vonnegut poisoned the reader with humanity as he felt all good writers should, according to Jerome Klinkowitz's work, *Kurt Vonnegut*. The reader should feel, as Vonnegut wishes his own children to feel, "that the news of the massacre of enemies [does] not fill them with satisfaction or glee". Thus, although the protagonist of *Slaughterhouse-Five* has little response to the scenes he sees, Vonnegut's own interpretation of these events is quite clear and should inform the reader's interpretation of Billy Pilgrim's experiences.

Vonnegut also introduces many of the themes and motifs of the novel in this chapter. For example, the ambiguous phrase, "So it goes," makes its first of many appearances after a mention of death. Time, the organizing (or, rather, disorganizing) principle of the novel, comes to the fore when Vonnegut waits in his Boston hotel room and the clocks behave srangely. In this book, described both death and time figure strongly.

For the reader who does not have a knowledge of Latin and German, a few translations, borrowed from Monica Loeb's mono-graph on *Slaughterhouse Five*, will assist the understanding of this chapter. First, the small Latin quote is adapted from Horace's *Odes*. As Vonnegut uses it, the phrase means, "Ah, me, the fleeting years are slipping by." Second, the paragraph of Goethe quoted in the context of Mary Endell's *Dresden, History, Stage, and Gallery*, ex-presses Goethe's "disgust at what the enemy has done to the Frauenkirche in particular". According to Monica Loeb's work, *Vonnegut's Duty-Dance with Death: Theme and Structure in* Slaughterhouse-Five, the purpose of this selection is to remind the reader of the cycle of destruction. It ties in strongly with Vonnegut's reference in the conclusion of this chapter to the Biblical tale of Sodom and Gomorrah. Dresden was not the first city to be utterly destroyed, with great loss of life: indeed, the firebombing of Dresden was not even the first time Dresden had been flattened by enemy forces. The question remains, of course, whether such destruction can be avoided.

Study Questions

1. What does Vonnegut say his breath smells like when he has been drinking?

2. What is strange about the set-up Mary O'Hare arranged for Vonnegut and her husband to talk about the war?

3. What does Vonnegut say World War II did for people?

4. Which previous occurrences of the destruction of cities does Vonnegut mention?

5. What is the only sound that disturbs the quiet following a massacre?

6. How does Vonnegut's boss in Schenectady compare to the other veterans Vonnegut meets there?

7. How does Vonnegut describe the carp in the Hudson river?

8. Whose death sets off the first "So it goes?"

9. How many books does Vonnegut refer to reading in this chapter?

10. Why does Vonnegut say he loves Lot's wife?

Answers

1. He says his breath smells like mustard gas and roses.

2. It is bright and uncomfortable, rather like an operating room.

3. World War Two has made everyone very tough.

4. Vonnegut reads about the flattening of Dresden in 1760, as well as the destruction of Sodom and Gomorrah.

5. The only exception to the general hush is the chirping of birds.

6. Vonnegut's boss is hostile and implies there is something wrong with him for not having been an officer in the war. The other veterans are kind men who hate war because of their experiences fighting.

7. Vonnegut says they "were as big as atomic submarines".

8. "So it goes" is said for the first time after Vonnegut mentions the Dresden taxi driver's mother who was burnt to ashes in the aftermath of the bombing of Dresden.

9. Vonnegut mentions five books in Chapter One.

10. Vonnegut loves Lot's wife, because her looking back to see Sodom and Gomorrah is "so human."

Suggested Essay Topics

1. Explain why Vonnegut has chosen to make this chapter the first of *Slaughterhouse-Five* rather than making it a preface.

2. Describe three different attitudes toward war described in this chapter. Who best epitomizes each view? How would you fit your own view into this scheme?

Chapter 2

New Characters:

Billy Pilgrim: *the time-travelling protagonist. He primarily varies between being a chaplain's assistant taken prisoner of war by the Germans and between his later life as a successful optometrist.*

Barbara Pilgrim: *Billy's worried daughter*

Tralfamadorians: *according to Billy, creatures from outer space who can see in the fourth dimension (time)*

Roland Weary: *a cruel American soldier who travels with Billy after the Battle of the Bulge*

Billy's mom (no name given): *in this chapter, a weak, old lady*

Summary

Billy Pilgrim is introduced as an involuntary time traveller. After a youth spent in Ilium, New York, Billy is sent to the battlefields of World War II in Europe. After the war, Billy finishes optical school, marries the daughter of his school's founder, and becomes a successful optometrist in Ilium. His grown daughter marries another optometrist, while his juvenile delinquent son straightens out to become a Green Beret and fight in Vietnam.

In 1968, Billy survives an airplane crash. His wife dies accidentally of carbon monoxide poisoning while he was recuperating in the hospital. Back at home, Billy slips off to New York City, where he gets on a radio talk show and announces that he had been kidnapped by space aliens from Tralfamadore, who kept him in a

zoo with his mate, the movie starlet Montana Wildhack. After being transported back to Ilium by his upset daughter, Billy proceeds to further aggravate his family by writing a letter to the local newspaper describing the Tralfamadorians in detail.

Billy is in the middle of writing his second letter to the paper. It describes the Tralfamadorian view of death, which is strongly tied to the Tralfamadorian view of time. Billy wants to try to help the people of earth by showing them how to see things the Tralfamadorian way. Billy's daughter finds him in the basement and berates him for making a fool of himself and his family.

The scene shifts to World War II, where Billy serves as a chaplain's assistant. Billy is sent to Luxembourg in December of 1944, where his regiment is destroyed in the Battle of the Bulge before Billy can even be properly uniformed.

Billy joins a group of three Americans wandering behind the German lines. Two of the men are scouts; the third is Roland Weary. Weary entertains himself by telling Billy about instruments and methods of torture, including ones of his own invention. Weary, who is warm and has energy to spare, runs back and forth between the scouts and Billy, pretending that he is in a war story.

Billy falls behind the group and has his first time-travelling experience, in which his father drops him into a pool, and Billy sinks to the bottom. He then travels to 1965, where he visits his mother in a nursing home, and to 1958, and 1961, where he passes out in the back of his car while looking for the steering wheel. He is awakened by Weary banging him against a tree.

Weary forces Billy back to the scouts, who have determined that they are being pursued. While Billy hallucinates, the scouts decide to ditch him and Weary. Weary is furious at Billy, whom he blames for the breakup of the noble fighting unit to which Weary imagined he belonged. As Weary is preparing to kick Billy in the spine, he realizes that he is being watched by a group of German soldiers and their dog.

Analysis

In the second chapter of *Slaughterhouse-Five*, the reader is finally introduced to the protagonist of the story, Billy Pilgrim, and given a quick summary of his life. After this, the main thrust of the

story might be expected to be Billy's conflicts with his daughter or his rise to success as a promoter of the Tralfamadorian way of life.

Yet, as this chapter shows, Vonnegut has not chosen to structure his novel around any expected form. The most important moment of Billy's life, the time he spent as a prisoner of war, will have more weight than Billy's life as an adult. Little time will be spent examining Billy's activities after he writes his second letter about the Tralfamadorians; rather, the narrative will travel widely over Billy's adult experiences as a resident of Ilium, New York.

Vonnegut, despite his self-characterization as a "trafficker in climaxes and thrills and characterization....and suspense"—that is, as a novelist—makes no attempts to adhere to such conventions of the novelistic form as building suspense. In Chapter One, Vonnegut announced the climax of the book will be the execution of Edgar Derby. The next chapter starts by describing the important events of Billy's life at the outset. Although the book will later explore many of these events in detail, the reader already knows what the outcome of the important events in Billy's life will be. There is also little suspense as to what will happen to Billy in Dresden, given the historical background Vonnegut provided in the first chapter.

This lack of suspense does, however, give a tremendous irony to the actions of the characters. In fact, the predetermined outcome of their lives makes it appear that they have little control over their lives—that they lack free will. The question of the existence of free will provides yet another theme of the novel, one which will be explicitly explored in Billy's encounters with the Tralfamadorians.

The traditional novel also naturalistically depicts a character's movement through time. Each event depicted in the novel follows one that proceeds it in time as well. Chapter Two casually ignores this conventional structure of time. Instead of treating time in a "linear" fashion, one that moves from start to finish in a straight line, *Slaughterhouse-Five* oscillates wildly between one moment in the protagonist's life and another.

Billy's life story is not difficult to follow, however. The links between events, often a sight or action that mimics one Billy has taken at some other period of his life, are similar to the

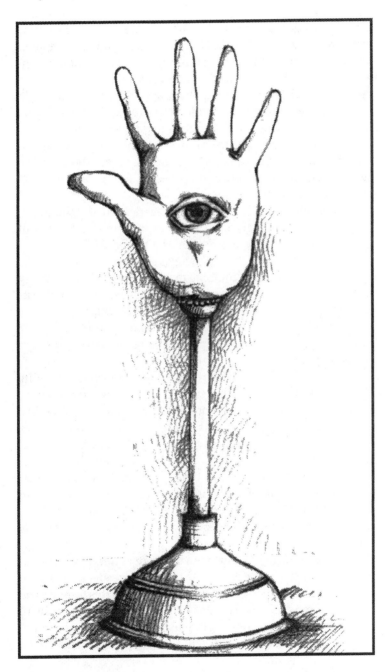

connections that a reader makes in his or her own mind to these sort of repetitions in real life. Vonnegut further aids the reader in reassembling the actual time of these episodes by providing chronological signposts at many of the interchanges. These usually take the place of references either to Billy's age or to the actual year in which the event takes place. As Monica Loeb details in *Vonnegut's Duty-Dance With Death*, rather than linking events together by time, Vonnegut has chosen to link them together through ideas and location. This is called the "'spatialization of time'." The result is a highly fragmented narrative, composed, as it were, of "'shrapnel bits'" that the reader has to reassemble.

Billy's being "unstuck in time," as he is described at the beginning of chapter two, is the most stated justification for the logic of this structure. Yet it is questionable whether or not Billy actually is a time traveller because Billy's judgement is itself questionable. Several textual elements combine to undermine Billy's credibility as a reliable interpreter of the novel's world. First, the narrative itself frequently indicates its doubt of Billy by inserting such phrases as "He says" (where it is set in its own paragraph for further emphasis). This immediately makes the reader question Billy's perception of reality.

Second, the description of the Tralfamadorians discredits Billy's sanity. While he may believe that he has been kidnapped by them, it is difficult to conceive of wise extraterrestrials shaped like plungers. The description seems designed by Vonnegut to evoke a response of hilarity instead of suspending the reader's disbelief enough to accept the inclusion of aliens in the novel's world. Finally, the moment when Billy's time travels initially occur, when he has apparently resigned himself to death in the chilly German forest, provides a plausible explanation for Billy's experiences: he is responding to a high-stress situation by escaping into a fantasy world.

In light of the doubt created in the reader's mind as to the actual nature of Billy's so-called "time travel," the reader must search for an explanation of why Billy experiences life in this fashion. The banality of most of the events of Billy's life and the simplicity of the prose used to describe them make them appear to be "true" within the context of the story. Since Billy appears to have lived a

normal (stress-free) life since the war's end (and since the Tralfamadorians only provide Billy with "insights" into his condition), his spasticity must have a purpose greater than providing an excuse for *Slaughterhouse-Five*'s disjointed narrative.

Given this fact, the reader should look further into what is causing Billy to travel through time. Its first occurrence in Billy's life seems unsurprising, given that he is fairly close to, and indeed ready for death. In later life, when he has decided to spread the wisdom of Tralfamadore, he has just been in a plane crash that left him with "a tremendous scar across the top of his skull," and his daughter with fears of damage to his brain. This, too, provides a plausible situation for Billy's bizarre beliefs and actions.

Yet Billy also had a "nervous collapse" a few years after the war. Sandwiched in between the other events of his life and given little attention in the narrative, Billy's mental breakdown should alert the reader to the unstable condition of his mind. What has caused it? What sets it off? While different interpretations are possible, the most obvious cause for the disturbance of Billy's mind must be the horrors he experienced and witnessed as a prisoner of war. This throws a different light on Billy's non-judgemental attitude toward his experiences as a prisoner of war. His mind appears to have been damaged by these events. The question will remain whether Billy ever regains his sanity, or if, indeed, his insanity provides him a point of view which is saner than that of most people. The reader should carefully consider this question when attempting to determine what the message of *Slaughterhouse-Five* is supposed to be.

Study Questions

1. What is the name of the fighting group to which Weary imagines he belongs?

2. How does Billy later find one of his army practice maneuvers to provide a Tralfamadorian type of adventure?

3. Why was Billy not missed while he was in the Tralfamadorian zoo?

4. Why does Billy say he did not talk about his adventures before the plane accident?

5. How do Tralfamadorians perceive time?

6. How do Tralfamadorians understand death?

7. What phrase is the Tralfamadorian response to death?

8. How does Billy's vocation parallel his purpose in propounding Tralfamadorian philosophy?

9. How does Billy's first time travel experience parallel his condition in real time?

10. Why do Billy and Weary surprise the German soldiers?

Answers

1. The group is called the Three Musketeers.

2. In later life, the experience of having his unit eat lunch after the men in it were pronounced "dead" struck him as a very Tralfamadorian experience.

3. Billy was taken through a time warp, so although he was on Tralfamadore for years, he was only gone from Earth for less than a second.

4. Billy thought the time was not ripe.

5. Tralfamadorians see time all at once, like a mountain range.

6. Tralfamadorians see death as just one bad moment, with plenty of other good moments of life existing alongside it.

7. "So it goes" is what the Tralfamadorians say about the dead.

8. Billy, who as an optometrist, helps people to see clearly, wants to provide vision for people's souls.

9. In both events, Billy is peacefully waiting for death.

10. They do not understand why one American is trying to kill another. They also do not understand why Billy is laughing.

Suggested Essay Topics

1. Explain the Tralfamadorian concepts of time and death.
    How do they compare to the Earthling understanding of
    these ideas? Why might Billy think that explaining the
    Tralfamadorian understanding of these two things might
    help his fellow Earthlings?

2. Examine Billy's hallucinations and time travelling experi-
    ences while he is a soldier. How do they illuminate his men-
    tal state? How do they compare to the fantasies of Roland
    Weary?

Chapter 3

New Character:

Wild Bob: *a colonel whose regiment has been destroyed*

Summary

After Weary and Billy are captured, they hear the shots of the guns that kill the scouts with whom they had been travelling. Weary is relieved of his weapons, as well as his boots, and is given a pair of wooden clogs.

After taking a brief side trip to his optometry practice in 1967, Billy rejoins the prisoners being marched away from the front. Billy returns to 1967, where he drives through the remains of Ilium's burnt out ghetto neighborhood. He listens to a Marine major give a speech in favor of increased bombings of North Vietnam at a Lions Club meeting. He drives home for his afternoon nap, which he spends weeping quietly.

Billy opens his eyes to find it is the winter wind that is making them run. Weary, who is marching near him, is also crying, but it is because his feet are being destroyed by his clogs. Billy marvels at the exciting scenery as he walks along, spotting corpses, weapons of mass destruction, and shot-out farmhouses.

The prisoners finally arrive at the railyards. One of the colonels there, who is dying of pneumonia, asks frantically for men from his annihilated regiment. In a delirium, he addresses Billy as if he were his entire body of troops, inviting them all to visit Wild Bob in Cody, Wyoming. Weary is the only member of Wild Bob's regiment at the railyards, but he is in great pain and does not respond to

Wild Bob's calls. Vonnegut adds that he and O'Hare were at the railyards.

The prisoners are loaded onto the boxcars according to their rank. A man dies in one of the boxcars. After dawdling in their own luxuriously outfitted car, the guards go to fetch the corpse, which is Wild Bob.

The prisoners wait two days for their train to depart, taking turns sleeping on the floor and sharing food. Billy falls asleep and time travels again to the night he was kidnapped by the Tralfamadorians.

Analysis

This chapter follows the two main threads of Billy's life: his capture by the Germans and subsequent march to the railyards with other prisoners of war, and his life as an optometrist in 1967.

While Billy is obviously under stress as a prisoner, Billy's adult life presents several anomalies that seem to indicate a problem below the surface contentment. First, he falls asleep at work, even while examining patients. This is possibly a sign of narcolepsy, a stress-triggered sleeping disorder. Second, Billy cannot make himself care about things, whether it is the future of optometry in Europe or the destruction of North Vietnam by bombing. Third, he is prone to unexplained crying fits. All of these problems indicate stifled emotions.

This combination of symptoms makes it seem doubtful that Billy has adjusted to civilian life as well as his commercial success would indicate. Instead, he seems to be repressing some terrible secret, which requires such tremendous effort to contain that it results in his emotional withdrawal from the world. Even Billy does not know why he cries. It is a mystery for the reader to solve, one that seems likely to illuminate Billy's flying saucer journey.

Billy's sanity during his experiences as a prisoner of war is highly questionable. His journey to the railyard is marked by frequent trips through time, which occur even while Billy is involved in some other activity. He also begins to see electric haloes around people's heads. These signs of mental distress make Billy's lack of response to the death and destruction he sees seem less likely to be caused by indifference than stress. In fact, his brain is

scrambling Billy's sensory input well enough for him to greet abuse with laughter and smiles, and to welcome the sight of the guards' home as heartily as that of a bullet-riddened farmhouse. Since Billy has no control over the events around him (as epitomized in the poem hung in his office), his brain seems to have decided to make every experience a pleasant one. The book will later label this a Tralfamadorian way of dealing with life.

Among the many criticisms of Vonnegut's writing is that his style is too simplistic. As William Allen says in *Understanding Kurt Vonnegut*, "It is easy to view Vonnegut as the simplest of writers—one who offers his readers short sentences, short paragraphs, cartoon-like characters, and lots of jokes"). Certainly it is true that Vonnegut's use of short paragraphs and incorporation of open space (and even drawings) makes it easy for the eye to follow his words across the page. As previously noted, this audience-friendly style of writing combined with Vonnegut's sales figures to confirm to many academic critics that his novels lack serious literary merit.

However, it must be observed that Vonnegut has made a conscious decision to write his novels in this fashion. As he said in an oft-quoted interview, "I'm not inclined to play Henry Jamesian games because they'll exclude too many people from reading the book...I have made may books easy to read, punctuated carefully, with lots of white space". In another interview quoted in Loeb's book, he said since the readers eyes don't get tired, "you get him [the reader] without him knowing it by making his job easy for him" Vonnegut wants his novels to be accessible to the general public.

Furthermore, in this age of television, Vonnegut has accepted that people have shorter attention spans. For this reason, his novels have generally been short, as well as frequently paragraphed. Additionally, Vonnegut has rejected pretentiousness and chosen instead to use a naturalistic language in his work. This combination of short, easy-to-read novels written in the vernacular has enabled Vonnegut's books to, as stated in *The Critical Response to Kurt Vonnegut*, "retain the middle class audience to whom the novel genre originally spoke".

Why should all of this matter to a writer? The answer lies in yet another interview, this one found in *The Vonnegut Statement*. In wondering why one should bother writing books when the people in power do not read them, Vonnegut responded, as mentioned earlier in this text, that one must catch people who are still open to ideas and "poison their minds with…humanity," in order to "encourage them to make a better world". This statement should be kept in mind when attempting to determine the "moral" of *Slaughterhouse-Five*. Vonnegut does not want people to give up like Billy and withdraw from the world; he wants them to take actions to improve the world.

In order to have any hope of having a positive effect on the world, Vonnegut must reach as many people as possible. This is the underlying reason for his so-called "naive" style. Thus, despite the fact that *Slaughterhouse-Five* ultimately challenges such notions as "the assumption of national innocence and intrinsic American worth," according to Klinkowitz, a philosophy which would repulse many readers, by coating his subversive notions in a layer of accessibility and humor, Vonnegut has been able to get readers to "swallow his sugar-coated pill", according to Loeb, and take in his ideas.

Despite its overt simplicity, critics feel *Slaughterhouse-Five* certainly qualifies as being sophisticated". First, the very ordinariness of the text's description of war scenes imbues them with more horror than complex metaphors, which would more than likely draw attention away from the event and toward artistic device— and its creator's cleverness. Furthermore, the reader cannot help but wonder why Billy Pilgrim is not reacting unfavorably to what he sees. He cannot possibly perceive so much death and destruction as commonplace. Additionally, the banality of Vonnegut's prose serves to further emphasize the banality of Billy's existence. The disconcerting effect this creates is to make Billy's outer- (and inner-) space adventures seem as commonplace as his time spent in the office, leaving the reader unsure if he is reading about reality or merely a crazy man's perception of reality. Thus, Vonnegut's style serves to add further depth to his protagonist.

Study Questions

1. In what context have the blue and white feet of this chapter's corpses previously appeared?

2. What precise phrase describes the condition of Weary's feet?

3. How do the actions of the teenaged German soldier toward Billy contrast to Weary's treatment of him?

4. What underlying misconception fuels Wild Bob's ranting?

5. How does Vonnegut humanize the German guards?

6. What heavenly visions does Billy have in this chapter?

7. What is ironic about Billy's lack of discussion at the Lions Club meeting he attends in this chapter?

8. How does the adult Billy's attitude toward his son's profession differ from what Vonnegut says he has inculcated in his sons?

9. What does the former hobo have to say about conditions on the boxcar?

10. Why was Billy thrown into a shrubbery by the Germans?

Answers

1. Chapter Two described Billy as having blue and white feet as he typed in the basement of his frigid house.

2. They are being turned into "blood puddings".

3. While Weary was ready to beat Billy senseless, the German boy helps Billy to his feet.

4. Wild Bob is still imagining that war is neat. He is essentially living in a war movie rather than in the reality of war.

5. Rather than shooting at Billy when he is seen looking out of the ventilator of his boxcar, the guard just wags his finger at him.

6. Billy sees Adam and Eve in a German soldier's boots and a little paradise inside the guard's boxcar.

7. Even though Billy has seen the tremendous destruction and suffering caused by the bombing of Dresden, he registers absolutely no response, spoken or unspoken, to the Marine major who gives a speech in favor of bombing North Korea back to the Stone Age.

8. While Billy tells the Marine major that he is proud of his Green Beret son, Vonnegut has said that he has told his sons never to take part in massacres.

9. He says things aren't so bad.

10. They wanted to stage an "actual capture" for a German reporter to photograph.

Suggested Essay Topics

1. Despite the fact that Billy is a prisoner of the Nazis, their actions are far more humane than the norm for World War II literature. Why does Vonnegut choose to depict the Nazis in this fashion? Compare the German soldiers to the Americans. How do their differences and similarities affect the message Vonnegut is trying to convey?

2. Explain the symbolic role of the hobo in this chapter.

Chapter 4

New Characters:

Paul Lazzaro: *a rabid American with a thirst for revenge*

Edgar Derby: *a kind, middle-aged American doomed to be shot for stealing a teapot*

Summary

Billy is unable to sleep the night after his daughter's wedding. He wanders around the house, knowing he is about to be kidnapped by the Tralfamadorians. He watches a movie in reverse time, then imagines it continuing from World War II all the way to Adam and Eve. After watching the movie in regular time, he goes outside and enters the space ship.

Billy asks why he has been taken. A Tralfamadorian tells him that the moment just is, and that there is no "why" to be asked. Billy is stuck like a bug in amber.

The acceleration of the Tralfamadorian ship sends Billy back to his boxcar. He wants to sleep, but his fellow prisoners refuse to let him lie among them because he thrashes in his dreams.

No food is given to the prisoners as they are transported across Germany. In the car ahead of Billy's, Roland Weary dies of gangrene. He tells everyone on his car that he wants Billy to be punished for killing him.

The prisoners finally arrive in a converted extermination camp and leave their boxcars. Billy is given a ridiculous overcoat.

In the camp, the prisoners are stripped prior to delousing. Among the men are Edgar Derby, who comforted Weary as he died, and Paul Lazzaro, who promised Weary he'd get Billy Pilgrim.

The shower sends Billy back to a happy moment in his infancy. Then he travels to his middle age, where he is playing a game of golf. In a moment of dizziness, he goes back to the spaceship, where he is strapped to a contour chair. The spaceship is heading for a time warp.

A Tralfamadorian tells Billy that he is on the spaceship because that is the way things have to be. When Billy asks if this means that the creature doesn't believe in free will, the Tralfamadorian responds that across the universe, only Earthlings believe in free will.

Analysis

This chapter follows young Billy up to his arrival in the prisoner-of-war camp in Germany, while simultaneously recounting the events surrounding Billy's kidnapping by the Tralfamadorians. In both of these story lines, Billy is being held against his will by kindly jailors.

Lawrence Broer finds many other parallels between Billy's experiences with the Tralfamadorians and his memories of being a prisoner of war. For example, Billy himself finds that the buildings look the same. Billy's reception in both places is also similar; he is laughed at by Germans and Tralfamadorians alike. Later, both of his prisons will be destroyed in an apocalyptic fashion. The primary difference between the two scenarios is, according to Lawrence R. Broer, that "in the case of his Tralfamadorian fantasy, Billy himself holds the keys to the locked doors of his mind".

The argument for Billy's flying saucer adventure being a delusion is great. The living situation in which he describes there, that of being in a zoo with an Earth woman as his mate, parallels the plot of a science fiction book he reads after the war. Furthermore, the woman who is chosen for his mate is a porn star—exactly the kind of woman a man living in a sexless marriage might fantasize about living with. While in a New York sex shop, Billy reads that his zoo mate Montana has disappeared and is presumed to be "wearing a cement overcoat" in the bottom of a bay. This is a clear example of reality intruding into Billy's fantasy. The only argument in favor of Billy not being delusional is his foreknowledge of his death; but as one critic put it, this could be a fantasy, too.

The main purpose of the existence of the Tralfamadorians in this novel (they previously appeared in *Sirens of Titan*) is to introduce a new philosophy. The primary component of Tralfamadorian philosophy is their understanding of time. Since they can see in four dimensions, they can view all moments in time simultaneously, like a mountain range. (By comparison, the human concept of time will later be described as that of a man strapped on a flatcar who sees the world flashing by through a tiny hole in a helmet.) With this type of vision, the Tralfamadorians can choose what exact moments they wish to admire, and as they tell Billy, they prefer to look at the good times.

This view of time has given the Tralfamadorians two other important beliefs. The first regards their view of death. The Tralfamadorians do not see death as a tragedy. As explained by Billy in chapter two, the Tralfamadorians believe a person only *appears* to die. Since Tralfamadorians can see all moments in time simultaneously, they see the moments in time when a person is alive as well as the moments in which he is dead. In this event, as in all others, they need only focus on the moments at which they enjoy looking. This is why a Trafalmadorian can say "so it goes" at the mention of a person's death: he can still enjoy the person being alive.

The second Tralfamadorian belief that is of importance to the book regards free will. Simply put, the Tralfamadorians do not believe that free will exists. People do what they have to in the ballet of time. All actions are predetermined: we are like insects frozen in amber. The theme of free will—or, rather, its non-existence in the life of Billy Pilgrim—runs subtly throughout *Slaughterhouse-Five*.

Why should free will be so important to this novel? The answer seems to hinge on its relationship to the firebombing of Dresden. There was absolutely no strategic benefit to be gained from destroying Dresden. The annihilation of such a beautiful city, in a manner guaranteed to result in massive, horrible civilian deaths (more died there than in Hiroshima), can therefore only be explained as an act of free will.

The question that remains is what lesson Vonnegut wants the reader to learn about free will. This is a matter of some debate among Vonnegut critics. The question is made more complex by

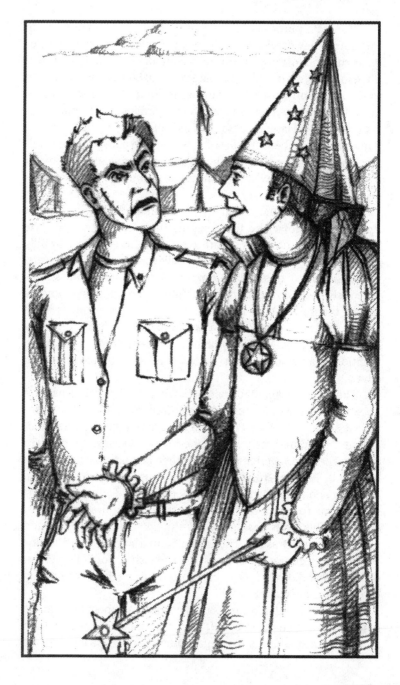

the identification of Vonnegut's view, which appears in the first and last chapter, with that of either Billy Pilgrim or the narrator. It has been said that Billy is Vonnegut, and they do share a well-documented similarity of appearance as well as experience. It has also been claimed that Vonnegut's view is identical to that of omniscient narrator of chapters two through nine. This argument hinges on all of the chapters' use of the Tralfamadorian phrase "so it goes."

Since the point of view of the narrative, with its "so it goes," seems to be Tralfamadorian, and Billy's attitude is also Tralfamadorian, the conclusion would be that Vonnegut also does not believe in the existence of free will. The lesson to be learned from *Slaughterhouse-Five* would therefore be not to be upset by the world's tragedies and to concentrate instead on the happy moments.

Yet while Billy may be aspiring to such a state of detachment, he still has his crying jags. While the omniscient narrator may be unmoved by people's deaths, Vonnegut, an active pacifist who remained horrified by Dresden long enough to hold its memory into the 1960s, clearly is not. Vonnegut's own opinion, and hence that of the novel, cannot therefore be to adopt the Tralfamadorian philosophy explained so vividly in the book.

Billy, the shell-shocked soldier, needs the lies of Tralfamadore to deal with the innumerable deaths he has witnessed and his own inability to control his life. His philosophy allows him to reach a state of bliss. However such massacres will continue if people believe they are inevitable. While wars may actually be as unstoppable as glaciers, to do nothing only encourages their proliferation. Adopting fatalism is not the lesson to be learned from *Slaughterhouse-Five*.

Study Questions

1. Where has the phrase "mustard gas and roses" previously appeared?

2. What promise does Paul Lazzaro make to Roland Weary before he dies?

3. Aside from crowding, what hardships do the Americans endure on their voyage to the prison camp?

4. How is Billy's coat different from everyone else's?

5. Give three details from this chapter that highlight the irony of Edgar Derby's eventual execution.

6. Why is Billy not allowed to sleep on the floor with everyone else?

7. How does the Tralfamadorian say his kind sees time?

8. What two people die on the way to the prison?

9. For what purpose was the German camp constructed?

10. What is the first question Billy has for the Tralfamadorian?

Answers

1. Vonnegut used this phrase to describe his own breath in Chapter One.

2. Lazzaro promises to punish Billy Pilgrim for causing Weary's death.

3. It is very cold outside, and they receive no more food.

4. Billy is the only person to receive a civilian's coat.

5. First, Derby had to pull strings to get to fight in the war. Second, his treatment of Roland Weary shows him to be a good man. Third, Derby is one of the few men who actually appears fit enough to be a soldier.

6. He kicks and makes noise in his sleep.

7. He says Tralfamadorians see time stretched out like the Rocky Mountains.

8. Roland Weary and the kindly bum both die.

9. It was intended to be a place for the extermination of Russian captives.

10. Billy asks, "Why me?"

Suggested Essay Topics

1. Examine the repetitive imagery of *Slaughterhouse-Five.* What is its structural role in the novel? Choose two repeating images and discuss their symbolic role.

2. Discuss the meaning of the backwards movie Billy watches while he waits for the flying saucer's arrival. What do Billy's extrapolations add to the role of this film in the book?

Chapter 5

New Characters:

Eliot Rosewater: *a patient next to Billy at the insane asylum*

Valencia Merble: *Billy's fiancee, and later wife*

Montana Wildhack: *Billy's mate in the Tralfamadorian zoo*

Summary

Billy reads *Valley of the Dolls* while he is aboard the spaceship. His captor explains to him the curious Tralfamadorian style of writing, which is like reading several telegrams at the same time.

Passing through a time warp sends Billy to two events on a family vacation in the West when he was twelve. Then he goes back to the prison camp. The Americans are led to a bright shed, from which a troop of Englishmen marches out to meet them. The Englishmen are in excellent shape. They have prepared a feast and entertainment for their American guests.

After setting his coat on fire and shocking the British with his miserable condition (and ridiculous coat), Billy watches a drag performance of *Cinderella* that makes him so hysterical he has to be carried out and given a shot of morphine. He is watched over in the prison hospital by Edgar Derby, who reads to him from *The Red Badge of Courage*.

Billy dreams, then time travels to 1948, where he is a patient at a mental ward in Lake Placid. In the bed next to Billy's is Eliot Rosewater, who also is finding life meaningless. Rosewater has brought with him his beloved collection of science fiction books

by Kilgore Trout. He has introduced Billy to them, and both of them have been using science fiction to help them reinvent their lives.

Billy hides from his mother underneath the bedcovers. She talks instead to Rosewater, telling him that Billy is engaged to a rich woman.

Billy wakes up in the prison hospital, where an Englishman is checking on him. He then returns to the asylum, where his fiancée, Valencia, is now visiting him. Rosewater talks to them about the Trout book he is reading.

Billy then travels to the zoo on Tralfamadore. While in the zoo, Billy is told that the Tralfamadorians will one day, accidentally, destroy the universe. The Tralfamadorians also tell Billy that they deal with such unpleasant moments by not looking at them. Instead, they look at enjoyable things, like the zoo. They think it's a philosophy Earthlings would do well to follow.

Billy goes to his wedding night. Valencia tells him how happy she is, then tries to talk to him about the war. Walking into the hotel bathroom, Billy comes back to the prison camp, where the Americans are sick with diarrhea.

The next morning, Paul Lazzaro shows up in the hospital with a broken arm. A German major visits the Englishmen there and reads to them from a monograph about the pitiful condition of American enlisted men. Billy regains consciousness in Ilium, where his daughter is still lecturing him.

He then travels to the zoo, where Montana Wildhack has just arrived. Although she is initially terrified, she grows to love Billy and they have delightful sex together. Billy wakes up in his bed in Ilium, where he remembers his daughter taking him after she discovered the furnace was broken. He has had a wet dream about Montana Wildhack.

The next day he goes back to his office for the first time since his trip to New York. His first patient is a boy whose father has just been killed in Vietnam. Billy tries to share his Tralfamadorian philosophy with the boy, whose mother tells the receptionist that Dr. Pilgrim is insane. His daughter comes back to the office and takes him home.

Analysis

This chapter is full of insights into Billy's character. Outstanding among the elements of his personality is Billy's lack of passion for life. He is a zombie, albeit a cheerful one. His existence is summed up in the words of the English officer who says that it must be nice to feel nothing and still get full credit for being alive. Billy's view improves as he adopts the attitude of the Tralfamadorians, who only want to feel pleasant emotions, as is shown by Billy's chosen epitaph. Billy manages his mind so that he can go from merely feeling nothing to seeing life as pleasant and empty of pain.

However, Billy's commitment to an asylum after the war shows that Billy was hurt and needed help. Like Rosewater, Billy suffers from the feeling that life is meaningless. Science fiction is supposedly helping Billy with his problems. This would only leave him needing to be loved and accepted—the desires shown in his giraffe dream—to be a truly happy man.

So why does Billy see marrying Valencia as a symptom of his insanity? Outwardly, it seems a means to provide Billy with the love he wants. But since Billy does not love Valencia and is not even attracted to her, the only reason he married her was to set himself up financially. By choosing money over love, Billy will certainly be able to fit in to a materialistic society. He will then be able to create meaning in his life through his possessions, at the expense of any possible emotional fulfillment.

In choosing this path, Billy shows that he has decided to deal with his troubles by running away from them. Science fiction books are not providing him with psychological insights, but rather a way to escape the horror of war and (later) the reality of his banal existence. Billy even refuses to air his war memories with his wife. Billy remains a kind person, but his choice of a shallow life (and his lack of intellect) will not allow him to deal with his war experiences in a therapeutic way. Ultimately, his subconscious' attempt to resolve his inner conflict will send him on a imaginary trip to another galaxy.

A further intriguing layer of *Slaughterhouse-Five* is its inclusion of the world of Kurt Vonnegut's other novels. First, Billy himself is from Ilium, New York, the setting of *Player Piano*, Vonnegut's first full-length novel. (It is generally assumed that Ilium is meant to be Schenectady, where Vonnegut worked for General Electric.) Second, many of the characters from Vonnegut's earlier novels reappear in *Slaughterhouse-Five*. Among them is Eliot Rosewater (of *God Bless You, Mr. Rosewater*) and Howard Campbell (the protagonist of *Mother Night*), as well as the time-travelling Tralfamadorians of *Sirens of Titan*. The cumulative, and somewhat humorous, effect of these intrusions is to make Billy appear to be travelling through yet a third fantasy: that of Vonnegut's fiction.

More important to the novel is Vonnegut's direct intrusion into the text. Both the omniscient narration of *Slaughterhouse-Five* and the use of a fictional protagonist seem necessary devices for Vonnegut to manage this subject. These devices allow Vonnegut to discuss his war experiences in a detached way. Vonnegut's clear identification of his own voice within the narrative establishes his existence as separate from it. His intrusions also give more power to the narrative by reminding the reader that much of what this book describes is not fiction but fact. This makes each quietly depicted scene of war leap into high relief in the reader's mind.

By switching back from third to first person, Vonnegut succeeds again in breaking the rules of the traditional novel form. Vonnegut simply does not allow the reader to relax into the usual state of suspension of disbelief. (This is the device which allows the reader to make sense of a "fiction" by telling himself that what he reads is real within the context of the story). Instead, Vonnegut plays games with the concept of fiction. He tells the reader that his story is "pretty much true," but Billy's adventures are clearly imaginary. At the same time, the novel's fantasy world intrudes into "reality" (in the autobiographical opening chapter) when the clocks in Vonnegut's hotel room begin to act strangely. Finally, Vonnegut interrupts the narrative by inserting himself directly into the novel. The cumulative effect is that Vonnegut slaps the reader back into an awareness of the nonexistence of the world which his mind has been inhabiting. This type of unconventional writing, which gives "attention to its own artificiality," is called "metafiction", as explained in William Rodney Allen's piece, *Understanding Kurt Vonnegut*. It is a further sign that Vonnegut is anything but a writer of simple tales.

Finally, Vonnegut's intrusion into his story invites a comparison between himself and his protagonist. Billy and Vonnegut are both creators of fantasy. But Billy is a man of little imagination. His fantasies seem to have arisen spontaneously from his subconscious mind in response to the tension of suppressing so many bad memories. He uses his fantasies to escape his troubles. Vonnegut, who is obviously more intelligent than his protagonist, has recast his troubles as fantasy in order to confront, and hopefully, subdue them. Denial might have been the easier choice, but Vonnegut has chosen instead to turn the evils he has experienced into a lesson for others.

Study Questions

1. What does Billy dream of when he is on morphine?

2. How does the scene with the punched prisoner parallel an experience Billy has with the Tralfamadorians?

3. What does Eliot Rosewater have to say about *The Brothers Kamazarov*?

4. While visiting Billy what does Valencia's chosen topic of conversation say about her personality?

5. What is the problem with the Bible as it stands, according to *The Gospel from Outer Space*?

6. At what two points does Vonnegut insert himself into the narrative of this chapter?

7. How does the universe end, according to the Tralfamadorians?

8. How is Montana Wildhack's body described?

9. Why was Paul Lazzaro's arm broken?

10. Why does Billy think he can make his young patient happy?

Answers

1. Billy dreams he is a giraffe.

2. Both prisoners ask, "Why me?" to which the German responds, "Why anybody?" and the Tralfamadorian, "Why anything?"

3. It used to contain everything there was to know about life, but it just wasn't enough anymore.

4. Valencia's discussion of silver patterns makes her appear to be very shallow.

5. The Bible teaches that it is okay to lynch people who have no connections, according to the alien narrator of Trout's book.

6. Vonnegut says that Billy's epitaph would be good "for me, too." In concluding the passage about the sick American soldiers, Vonnegut says of one, "That was I. That was me. That was the author of this book."

7. An experimental Tralfamadorian jet fuel blows up the universe.

8. She is described as having baroque detailing, like the buildings of Dresden before they were bombed.

9. He was trying to steal cigarettes from one of the Englishmen.

10. If the little boy can grasp Billy's philosophy of death, he'll understand that he can see his father any time he wants to.

Suggested Essay Topics

1. It has been said that *Slaughterhouse-Five* is written in a circular pattern. Find evidence to substantiate this claim within the text. How would you describe the structure of this novel?

2. Does Billy appear to be maturing or changing over the course of his life? Discuss his character as shown by the novel. If Billy is not changing, what is moving the text?

Chapters 6 and 7

Summary

Billy returns, confused, to his German prison. He finds himself strangely drawn to his coat, which appears to contain two small lumps within the lining.

The Englishman who broke Paul Lazarro's arm returns to check on him. Lazarro says he is going to have him killed someday. After the other man leaves, Lazarro tells Billy that he is going to have him killed after the war, too.

Billy knows that his death is going to occur in 1976, after he gives a speech about Tralfamadore in Chicago. At this time, Billy has become very popular. He is shot by a laser gun wielded by Paul Lazarro, who has been hiding in the press box.

Billy comes back to life in 1945. He and his two companions leave the hospital and go into what used to be the Englishmen's theater. An Englishman tells the Americans they are going to be leaving the camp. They will be sent to Dresden. Fortunately, they don't need to worry about being bombed, because Dresden engages in no significant war industries.

The Americans, feeling much better, leave for Dresden. They find the city amazingly beautiful. Vonnegut says it looks like Oz. It is the only big city in Germany that has not suffered a bombing attack.

Billy, looking ridiculous, leads the parade of Americans into the town. He knows it is going to be bombed in about a month. He is verbally abused by a German surgeon for his appearance. Billy wields the mysterious contents of his coat at the man, which turn out to be dentures and a two carat diamond.

The Americans are taken to the mostly empty slaughterhouse that will be their new home. They will be staying in the fifth building, which is called Slaughterhouse-Five.

Chapter Seven starts in 1970, as Billy boards a plane full of other optometrists. Billy knows it is going to crash. As the plane flies along, Billy goes back to being slammed against a tree by Weary.

The plane crashes, killing everyone but Billy and the copilot. Billy's skull is fractured. Thinking he is back in World War II, he tells his rescuers to return him to Slaughterhouse-Five. He is taken to a hospital, where he receives brain surgery. The next two days he dreams furiously.

In Dresden, Billy and Derby spend the month before the city's destruction, working in a malt syrup factory. Billy eats the nutritious syrup. He shares it with Edgar Derby, who is working outside of the factory. This makes Derby cry.

Analysis

These two, brief chapters follow Billy from the prison camp to the month he spends in Dresden before it is bombed, including information about the plane crash mentioned in the beginning of the story, as well as Billy's eventual death.

While Billy's war experiences seem real enough, his perception of time and belief in flying saucers is quite odd. Yet Billy is odd even as a soldier. In earlier chapters he has seen people haloed with Saint Elmo's fire; he hears the objects in the coat calling to him and even giving him advice.

As the book develops, the timing of Billy's time traveling episodes seems more suspect. In Chapter Five, he time travels when asked by Valencia to recall an unpleasant memory, and in Chapter Seven, Billy time travels in response to his precognition of the plane's demise. Stress seems a possible trigger for Billy's time travel, but it may not be the only reason they occur.

The exact nature of these episodes remains ambiguous. Chapter Deven says Billy's time travels are true, which must be the case if he can see his death and predict a plane crash. Yet the fact that Billy's skull is fractured in the wreck and that he undergoes brain

surgery casts aspersions on his reliability. It is entirely possible that Billy hallucinates his death in response to the head trauma he experiences as a result of the plane crash. Even his daughter questions the timing of the plane crash and Billy's decision to preach the Tralfamadorian way. Yet the text says his time travels are true and treats Billy's seemingly psychic moments as unremarkable. It is therefore up to the individual reader to interpret the evidence and form his or her own conclusion about Billy's perceptions.

During these chapters, Edgar Derby has remained generally static. Most of his actions have been perfectly in keeping with his description in the text, which says he is a man "mournfully pregnant with patriotism and middle age and imaginary wisdom". In light of this description, the only action he takes, which makes him come alive, is when he cries when Billy gives him a spoon of malt syrup. He may be realizing that the truth of war is going to be suffering rather that noble actions. Billy's gift is selfless and kind, and Derby's response acknowledges that in times of war this is the type of action that is truly remarkable.

Study Questions

1. Does Billy get committed to an asylum after the incident in his optometry office?

2. What does Paul Lazarro say is the sweetest thing in life?

3. Why does Billy take Cinderella's silver boots?

4. What animal disease is used to describe Paul Lazarro?

5. Why are the Dresdeners the color of putty?

6. What mistake does Billy make after the plane crash?

7. Which of the "millions of things" that Billy dreams after his operation are true?

8. What sarcastic comment does the cook in the communal kitchen of the slaughterhouse make to Billy, Derby, and their 16-year-old guard?

9. What benefit does working at the malt syrup factory have?

10. Why are there spoons hidden all over the factory?

Answers

1. He is not committed. His Tralfamadorian philosophy apparently becomes very popular some time between the publication of his first letters and 1976.

2. He says that revenge is the sweetest thing.

3. His own shoes have been nearly destroyed.

4. Lazarro is described as "fizzing with rabies." If he were a dog, he would have been shot.

5. They have been living off potatoes for two years.

6. He thinks he is back in World War II.

7. According to the text, the true things he dreams were time-travel.

8. She says that all of the real soldiers are dead.

9. The syrup is very nutritious and good to eat.

10. It is illegal to eat the syrup.

Suggested Essay Topics

1. Discuss the religious imagery in *Slaughterhouse-Five*. Is Billy supposed to be a Christ figure? What is the purpose of the numerous references to Adam and Eve?

2. The comment that Billy dreamed true things after his brain surgery is highly relevant in the interpretation of Billy's time travel experiences. What does it mean when the text says that his time travel experiences are true? How does this affect your interpretation of the underlying time structure of this novel and Billy's reliability as an interpreter of reality?

Chapter 8

New Characters:

Howard W. Campbell, Jr.: *an American Nazi propagandist*

Kilgore Trout: *a reclusive science fiction author*

Maggie White: *a beautiful, if simple, woman married to an optometrist*

Robert: *Billy's son, the future Green Beret*

Summary

Howard Campbell comes to the American prisoners. He wants to recruit them to fight against the Russians. He bribes the weary, undernourished men with promises of good food.

Surprisingly, Edgar Derby stands against Campbell's poisonous promises. He says that the Americans are going to unite with the Russians to crush Nazism. Then the air-raid siren starts to sound. All the men, including Campbell, hide in a meat locker far under the ground. However, no bombs fall, as they aren't scheduled to fall until the next day.

That night, Billy returns to the argument with his daughter. She expresses anger at Kilgore Trout, whom she blames for her father's problems. Trout is living in Ilium, where he works as a circulation manager for the local newspaper. Billy meets him in 1964. Billy is as amazed to find Trout as Trout is amazed to find someone who has read his books. Billy invites Trout to his eighteenth wedding anniversary party.

Because he is the only person at the party who is not an optometrist, Trout is a great hit. He tells Maggie White all sorts of lies
about his work. The optometrist barbershop quartet begins to sing
a song which upsets Billy so much people think he is having a heart
attack. It reminds Billy that he has been keeping a secret inside
himself, although he can no longer remember what it is. Trout accuses Billy of having seen through a time window, which Billy denies. Billy then hands Valencia the ring he bought her for an
anniversary gift.

Curious about Billy's reaction, Trout follows him around the
house until the quartet starts to sing again. This bothers Billy so
intensely that he has to leave the party. He runs upstairs, where he
finds Robert sitting on the toilet with his electric guitar. Billy leaves
him and goes into his bedroom.

Billy tries to understand why the quartet bothered him. The
effort brings up a crystal clear memory. The American prisoners
spent the night in the meat locker while Dresden was destroyed
and its population burnt within their shelters. When the guards
and the Americans emerged the next day, the burnt out city was
like the surface of the moon. The expressions of the four Germans
as they silently huddled together, making one face and then another, was identical to that of a barbershop quartet.

On Tralfamadore, Montana Wildhack is very pregnant. She asks
Billy to tell her a story, and he relates the tale of the German barbershop quartet. He tells her about the little logs that were actually people scattered about the ruins of Dresden.

The group has to leave the city in search of food. They are shot
at by American fighter planes as they walk over the mountains of
rubble. They make it to a suburb where an inn is open, expecting
refugees from Dresden. The guards tell the innkeeper that, after
half a day's travel, they have not seen one living person.

Analysis

At long last, Chapter Eight arrives at the bombing of Dresden,
the moment which the reader hopes will never come. In a certain
sense, there has been little suspense about the event. The text has
constantly pointed out people who would die in the firestorm and
discussed the temporal nature of the city's beauty.

Yet each reminder of coming death and destruction has only made the actual event more painful to read about. The reader has formed a relationship with the embarrassed girls in the shower and the worn down prison cook. Sympathy has been developed for the general population of Dresden, who have gone pale from living on potatoes. The reader can feel no sense of righteous victory over the forces of evil. In fact, one cannot help but wish a *deus ex machina* to provide a happy ending, but *Slaughterhouse-Five* gives no such relief. The scene is unbearably, heartbreakingly bleak.

Derby's speech to Campbell provides an interesting commentary on the action of the text at this point, as well as insight into Vonnegut's political views. Campbell himself is the protagonist of Vonnegut's *Mother Night*. As presented in *Slaughterhouse-Five* he is basically the same character as in *Mother Night*—an American working as a Nazi propagandist. *Mother Night* has much more detail, of course: in it, Campbell is also spying for the American forces and suffering a terrible identity crisis.

In *Slaughterhouse-Five*, Campbell attempts to recruit American P.O.W.s into his "Free American Corps." According to Monica Loeb, although there was no Free American Corps, there was a "Free British Corps" which was organized along similar lines and was similarly unsuccessful. Contrasted against this vile man, Derby appears to be a hero, to become a real "character," as the text praises him.

Yet Derby's speech is the height of irony. He praises America as the land of "freedom and justice and opportunities and fair play for all"). He says that any of the American soldiers would be willing to die for their country's ideals. However, the next day, the American sense of justice turns a blind eye to the city of Dresden, which is destroyed out of pure malice. The bombing of Dresden is a ringing denial of the existence of justice as a keystone of American government.

Perhaps, however, this "slip" can be excused as an excess of war. But the irony of Derby's speech is extended if one has read Vonnegut's *God Bless You, Mr. Rosewater* (1965), which immediately preceded *Slaughterhouse-Five*. *God Bless You, Mr. Rosewater* describes an American system in which "opportunities and fair play" are a myth that keeps the poor quiet. The Campbell propaganda pamphlet quoted in Chapter Five (on the American soldier as a product of the pathetic condition of American society) is essentially a distillation of the themes of the earlier novel. In various speeches he has made, Vonnegut has said that he himself does not believe that the American system provides what it is supposed to, and that it would be better supplanted by socialism. While the Campbell pamphlet could be taken as a bitter propaganda piece by a Nazi sympathizer, it is full of analyses that disturb because they ring true, and in doing so show the lie of the American Dream. Derby may have become a "character" at this moment in the novel, but he is still only full of "imaginary wisdom."

In this section of *Slaughterhouse-Five*, the text makes an oddly self-aware comment about what many have seen as a failure in Vonnegut's style. The text says, "There are almost no characters in this novel, and almost no dramatic confrontations, because most of the people in it are so sick and so much the listless playthings of enormous forces".

Earlier, Vonnegut had described himself as a "trafficker in ... characterization," one of the many tasks one must undertake as a writer. Yet most of the characters in this book are both flat and static. As Monica Loeb says, "Vonnegut does not develop in-depth characters, but he prefers sketchy, flat, almost stereotyped characters". This trait was most fully pronounced in Vonnegut's first work, *Player Piano*, but it seems odd that almost twenty years later he would write a book in which even the protagonist is not a fully developed character .

There is little doubt, however, that Vonnegut's underdeveloped characterization has been a choice of style. On one hand, it is part of Vonnegut's simple or "naive" style. The characters are defined succinctly through their epithets ("poor, doomed Derby") and symbolic names (the overweight, tiresome Roland Weary). Stanley Schatt, author of *Kurt Vonnegut, Jr.*, finds Vonnegut's simplification of characters a helpful device to keep readers focused on the novel's ideas. For example, Weary's out-of-touch fantasies prove Mary O'Hare's belief that war books and movies glamorize the depressing truth of the matter. In this way, Vonnegut imitates his character Trout, of whom he says (in the guise of omniscient narrator), "Only his ideas were good".

Yet Vonnegut's sketchy characters are but a further proof of his skill as a modern writer. Allen points out that Vonnegut's output during this time was firmly within the aegis of the "exploded novel," which rejected all of the elements Vonnegut described in Chapter One as a writer's stock-in-trade. (Vonnegut will proceed to satirize the death of the novel in Chapter Nine, in which a critic declares the novel of primary use as a device for interior decorating). Vonnegut writes outside of the novel tradition, which focuses on creating realistic characters with psychological depth. Vonnegut's comment about the lack of characters in his novel is yet another metafictive stab at the novel tradition: the "enormous forces" playing with his characters is no less than the author himself. Vonnegut is announcing his presence by playfully reminding the reader that his characters have no free will, and that the forces that manipulate characters in books are always beyond their control.

Kilgore Trout, Vonnegut's most popular recurring character, also makes his appearance in this chapter. As an unsuccessful author of science-fiction books, Trout is often considered to be Vonnegut's alter-ego. Trout's remarks and the summarized plots of his books allow Vonnegut, Schatt explained, to "comment on the major themes of the book, thereby tightening the structure". While Trout may provide some motion in the plot as a character, he is far more useful (and more frequently used in the body of Vonnegut's fiction) as a source of pithy plots that critique American society. Trout's writings should never be considered irrelevant within the context of Vonnegut's novels.

Study Questions

1. What detail about the hog barn shows how intense the firestorm that engulfed Dresden must have been?

2. What is Campbell's final argument in favor of fighting the Russians?

3. Who does Barbara blame for Billy's problems?

4. How does Trout's book "The Gutless Wonder" recall Billy's son, Robert?

5. Why does the narrator claim there are few to no characters in this story?

6. How did the troop of Americans come to have only four guards?

7. What episode immediately follows Billy's recollection of the painful memory of Dresden?

8. How does Billy's response to the barbershop quartet reflect a conversation he had with Valencia on their wedding night?

9. How is Billy's survival given a further component of randomness on the march to the inn?

10. What is odd about the innkeeper's kindness to the American prisoners?

Answers

1. The fire was hot enough to leave "dollops of melted glass" on the ground.

2. He says that the Americans are going to have to fight the Communists "sooner or later."

3. Barbara blames Kilgore Trout.

4. Billy's son is a Green Beret in Vietnam, presumably dropping jellied gasoline on people or committing some similar atrocities.

5. There are few characters in the book because the characters in it are "so sick and so much the listless playthings of enormous forces" (140). This, the narrative adds, is one of the main effects of war.

6. The others left to be with their families.

7. Billy's memory of Dresden directly precedes a scene in the zoo with Montana.

8. Valencia had said to Billy that she thought he was full of secrets, which he denied. Now he discovers that he has been keeping secrets, but he can't remember what they are.

9. Billy's group nearly misses being shot by American fighting planes out "mopping up."

10. Given that the Allies have just destroyed Dresden and all of the people in it, it might have been more appropriate for the innkeeper to abuse the men instead of giving them food and a place to stay.

Suggested Essay Topics

1. Discuss the books of Kilgore Trout summarized in this chapter. How do they add to and support the themes of *Slaughterhouse-Five*?

2. Trace the sequence of Billy's time travels in this section. Although is not supposed to be controlling them, what psychological desires might be motivating his transfers?

Chapters 9 and 10

New Characters:

Bertram Copeland Rumfoord: *a history professor writing on Dresden*

Lily Rumfoord: *Rumfoord's trophy wife*

Summary
After she hears Billy's airplane has crashed, the hysterical Valencia rushes to the hospital, ripping the exhaust system off her car in an accident en route. Immediately after arriving, she is overcome by carbon monoxide poisoning. Shortly thereafter, she dies.

Billy is still unconscious. He is sharing a room with Bertram Rumfoord. Rumfoord's wife, Lily, brings Bertram books for the history of the United States Army Air Corps in World War II that he is writing. Rumfoord makes Lily read Truman's statement on the necessity of bombing Hiroshima.

Although Billy finally regains consciousness, he says little and is believed to be a vegetable. Rumfoord finds him to be disgusting and wonders out loud why the doctors don't let Billy die.

Rumfoord is having problems with his book because the parts on Dresden are going to be new. The Air Force and the American government had previously attempted to keep their success in Dresden a secret from the American public. After Rumfoord expresses his frustration to Lily, Billy says that he was there.

For a long time Rumfoord refuses to acknowledge that Billy is addressing him instead of echoing him. Billy finally speaks to him

after a long silence, but Rumfoord doesn't believe Billy was in Dresden.

Billy time travels to Dresden, where he is riding around in a wagon with some other Americans, looking for souvenirs. Billy is supremely happy dozing in the wagon. He is awakened by the voices of a middle aged German couple crooning to the abused horses. They get Billy out of the wagon and show him the horses' miserable condition. This makes Billy cry for the very first time in the war.

After questioning Billy, Rumfoord finally accepts that Billy was in Dresden. Rumfoord attempts gruffly to sympathize with Billy, while maintaining the necessity of Dresden's destruction. Billy agrees with everything Rumfoord says, adding that he learned that everything has to happen the way it does while he was on Tralfamadore.

Barbara takes Billy home later that day. He sneaks out and goes to New York City with the intention of spreading the good news about Tralfamadore. While he is there, Billy is drawn into an adult book store by some books by Kilgore Trout displayed in its window. The one Billy first reads turns out to be one he read long ago. It is about a man and woman who are kidnapped from Earth and put on display in an extraterrestrial zoo.

Billy also picks up an old girly magazine with a story about Montana Wildhack. Billy knows Montana is back in the zoo with their baby and not dead, as the magazine says she is.

That night, Billy manages to get on the panel of a radio show. When he finally is allowed to speak, he talks about his outer space adventures.

Back at his hotel, after being kicked out of the studio, Billy travels to Tralfamadore. He tells Montana, who is feeding their baby, about his trip to New York. She notices that the Tralfamadorians are playing with the clocks again. The chapter ends with an illustration of Montana's necklace and its enigmatic slogan.

Vonnegut resumes the narrative, ticking off the deaths of Robert Kennedy, Martin Luther King, numerous Vietnamese, and his father. Vonnegut says that he would not be overjoyed if Billy was right and it were true that everyone really lives forever. He's glad he has so many nice moments to visit. High among them is his trip back to Dresden with Bernard O'Hare.

Billy travels back to Dresden, where he, as well as O'Hare and Vonnegut, is pressed into service by German soldiers to dig out bodies from the rubble. They find many little pockets full of well-preserved corpses. Eventually the condition of the corpses deteriorates, and instead of being removed they are cremated on the spot.

During this time, Edgar Derby is shot for the theft of a teapot.

Finally, World War Two is over. Billy is free. He walks out into the spring air. A bird chirps to him.

Analysis

Chapters Nine and Ten bring *Slaughterhouse-Five* to an enigmatic conclusion. Structurally, it is a confusing ending because it seems that the book has reached a predictably happy ending in Chapter Nine, which ends with Billy at home with his family on Tralfamadore. The idea that this forms the conclusion of the fictional section of *Slaughterhouse-Five* is supported by Vonnegut's initial domination of Chapter Ten, which seems like a disguised post-script matching the introductory Chapter One.

The moment of peace is shattered, though, as Billy is reinserted in the story at the very moment Vonnegut seems as if he is going to reminisce about his trip to Dresden with Bernard O'Hare. However the climax of the book has not yet been reached, according to Vonnegut's outline in Chapter One: Edgar Derby has not yet died at the hands of a firing squad. More action seems ready to follow.

However the rest of Chapter Ten is quite relaxed. The moment of Derby's death receives no attention; it just happens, and is not described. It is difficult to conceive of this short paragraph as the climax of *Slaughterhouse-Five*.

Has Vonnegut, then, tossed out the climax along with the other elements of the novel? Although an argument could be constructed in support of this statement, *Slaughterhouse-Five* does reach a climax. The exact point is a matter of some dispute. Stanley Schatt makes a strong argument in favor of the climax occurring when Billy finally recollects the firebombing after the sight of the barbershop quartet affects him so strangely. As Schatt explained, "It is only after Billy has faced the past that he is able to return to Dresden and live through the holocaust once more."

Yet Schatt's interpretation seems to assume that Billy's recollections of Dresden appear in his life after the war in the sequence that they occur in the novel; that is, that Billy has been moving toward remembering the entire period of his imprisonment, but has only been able to proceed toward the firebombing. This is contradicted when Valencia mentions on her wedding night that she had overheard Billy discussing with her father Derby's death, which happened after the firebombing.

Billy has completely suppressed his memory of the war in order to continue his life. He denies his memories to Valencia and, as time goes by, to himself. He has completely lost himself in "trying to construct a life that made sense from things [he] found in gift shops". Valencia accepts that Billy gives her rings instead of real intimacy, because she, too, is hopelessly materialistic.

Schatt is right to say that "the firebombing is at the center of Billy's consciousness and is much more real to him than his shallow life as an optometrist in Ilium, New York". For this reason, Billy needs to accept his memories to make himself whole. This need is shown in Billy's fantasies about Tralfamadore and the sexy wife he has there. Montana, who is able to accept Billy's time-travelling (which is how he understands what he is experiencing), provides a rapt audience for Billy's war experiences. In contrast, Valencia would have been disappointed to find they are not glamorous.

Billy's memories have been trying to fight their way back to his conscious mind for years, as his inexplicable weeping fits show. Billy's first move toward wholeness would therefore be to acknowledge his experiences. He finally manages to do so (with a real person) when he tells Bertram Rumfoord, "I was there." This is the climax of the book. Unfortunately, the effort to integrate so much cruelty into a unified system of understanding life is more than Billy can undertake, and he instantly retreats into Tralfamadorian fatalism (read: insanity) because of his inability to integrate his experiences with his gentle personality. Like Derby, Billy becomes a character in a moment of confrontation. It is a point that shows he has grown as a person. While he may also be mad, his future popularity shows that there are many people who may turn to such a simplistic philosophy to explain a world so inexplicably cruel.

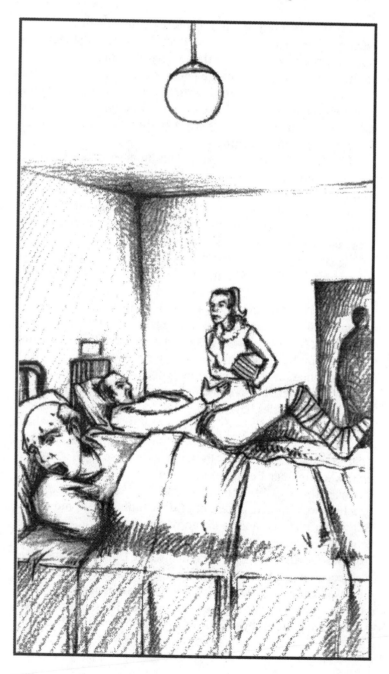

Does *Slaughterhouse-Five* have a moral to match its climax? Vonnegut's own comments in the first chapter argue against the existence of a moral to this story. He says that there is "nothing intelligent to say about a massacre." The birds' chirping says "all there is to say," which must be, according to the preceding sentence—nothing.

Or is it? "Poo-tee-weet" is used in Vonnegut's fiction a number of times. In *God Bless You, Mr. Rosewater*, it is like an exclamation point attached to the protagonist's sudden realization of how to extract himself from the trap set for him by his family and their lawyer. Schatt says that in this instance, and in every other, the bird's chirp represents "the cool, detached way to deal with a catastrophe". This is the same interpretation that many critics have given to the phrase "So it goes." This interpretation holds that the moral of *Slaughterhouse-Five* is to remove oneself from feeling the pain of the world, as there is nothing one can do to stop it.

Robert Uphouse, however, points out the contrast of the bird's song with the destruction that lies around it. Given Billy's need to cushion himself from horror in later life, Uphouse finds "Poo-tee-weet" to be a reminder of the human capacity for dealing with death through the imagination, as Billy and Vonnegut do.

Yet this explanation also seems unsatisfactory, since Billy's imagination leads him astray. It seems better to turn for an interpretation to Vonnegut himself, who says in Chapter One that after so much horror has been wrought in the world, "everybody is supposed to be dead, to never say anything or want anything ever again." But the birds' still cheerful songs show the dogged, perhaps even irritating, persistence of life amidst death. Their presence contradicts the finality of the situation, much as Billy's wagon contradicts its coffin shape by being green. "Poo-tee-weet", explained in *The Critical Response to Kurt Vonnegut*, cannot help but be a sign of hope within a "never-ending cycle of regeneration and destruction" .

Does Vonnegut have a moral? He might say he does not, but his frequently quoted statement that the role of an artist is to be a "canary in a coal mine" encourages the reader to probe the text for its message. A message can indeed be found, one that was most relevant when one remembers that this book was written during

"the nadir of America's self-confidence during the Vietnam war years", as stated in Klinkowitz's *Kurt Vonnegut*. The message is found by examining the ideas expressed by a few of Vonnegut's cardboard characters and keeping in mind that the characters themselves are designed to express ideas more than Vonnegut's mastery of psychological insight.

The character which enables Vonnegut to give a message to his story is Bertram Rumfoord. Rumfoord is the best-developed of a series of characters who glorify war, such as the Marine major, Roland Weary, and the British prisoners. Vonnegut makes Rumfoord a very unsympathetic man. Rumfoord is the kind of man who uses people as objects without regard for their feelings. He married his wife to show the world that he is a "superman," and he thinks that Billy should be turned over to a "veterinarian or a tree surgeon," implying that they would do the right thing by killing him.

Most damning is Rumfoord's attitude toward Dresden. Vonnegut has described it as a fairy city, as enchanting as Oz, full of people that the reader feels are as human as him or herself. When Rumfoord defends its destruction, the reader cannot help but be appalled. Like the former lieutenant colonel Vonnegut describes in Chapter One, Rumfoord is unlikely to have done much actual fighting or suffering, and he certainly has little feeling of kinship towards other humans. This allows him to see the Dresden raid as a "howling success" while ignoring its cost. Like the robots in Trout's *The Gutless Wonder*, Rumfoord has "no conscience, and no circuits which would allow [him] to imagine what would happen to people on the ground". He is the embodiment of the "myopic morality of all apologists for war," according to Schatt.

Vonnegut puts the lie to the statement "it had to be done." Coming out of the mouth of a despicable man like Rumfoord, the words are as foul as vomit. Billy's acquiescing response that everything has to be done as it is done—as the little green men taught him—slaps Rumfoord's ridiculous logic back in his face. It is clear that nothing has to be the way it is, whether in Dresden, Hiroshima, Dachau, or Vietnam. Choices are made at every point along the way that should be made with humanity, rather than excused with empty phrases.

"The real horror is that events such as Dresden continue to occur and no one seems appalled," as stated in *Critical Essays on Kurt Vonnegut.* The message of *Slaughterhouse-Five*, then, is to reject the lie "it has to be done," in war or elsewhere. Vonnegut is a canary in a coal mine, warning us that to let this attitude pass unchallenged, to deny that there are moral questions to be asked, to passively accept that history cannot be altered is to let atrocities happen again and again.

Study Questions

1. How do the aliens from Zircon-212 manipulate their human captives?
2. When did Billy previously read *The Big Board*?
3. What does the wagon Billy rides in look like?
4. What is the topic of the panel Billy sneaks into?
5. What killed the Maori soldier?
6. Where has the message on Montana's necklace previously appeared?
7. Why is Barbara glassy-eyed when she comes to visit her father in the hospital?
8. Why does Rumfoord say the Air Force wanted to cover up the bombing of Dresden?
9. Which historical personage do the Tralfamadorians find fascinating?
10. Where has the special picture the owners of the bookstore kept behind the counter previously appeared?

Answers

1. They make the humans think that they are investing in stocks for them back on Earth.
2. He read it when he was in the mental ward of the veterans' hospital.
3. It is green and coffin shaped.

4. The panelists have gathered to discuss the death of the novel.

5. He died of the dry heaves.

6. It was the motto on the wall of Billy's office.

7. She has been put under sedation because of the death of her mother and collapse of her father.

8. He says that the bombing was kept a secret because of the "bleeding hearts."

9. The Tralfamadorians are very sympathetic to the philosophy of Charles Darwin.

10. It is the same picture that Roland Weary was carrying around with him in Germany.

Suggested Essay Topics

1. The meaning of the bird's chirp at the end of *Slaughterhouse-Five* is a matter of much debate. How do you interpret it? Is it the embodiment of the "moral" of this novel?

2. Discuss Billy's experiences on Tralfamadore. What do they say about Billy's unmet psychological needs?

Sample Analytical Paper Topics

The following paper topics are designed to test your under-standing of the book as a whole and analyze important themes and literary devices. Following each question is a sample outline to help you get started.

Topic #1

The argument that the message of *Slaughterhouse-Five* is to withdraw from the world has occasionally been predicated on the assumption that Vonnegut believes man is essentially evil. What view does *Slaughterhouse-Five* take of the nature of man—that we are good, evil, or amoral? How does the firebombing of Dresden fit in to your conclusion?

Outline

I.   Thesis Statement: *Although* Slaughterhouse-Five *depicts man as naturally good, the military's code of amorality strips away natural compassion.*

II. Humane actors

    A.   Edgar Derby

    B.   German civilians

    C.   German soldiers at rail yard

III. Cruel actors

    A. "Rabid" Paul Lazzaro

    B. German soldier at prison camp

    C. Bertram Rumfoord

IV. Dresden

    A. Residents are sympathetic

    B. Lack of morality in Trout's *The Gutless Wonder*

    C. Bombing only possible when sympathy "circuits" are cut

Topic #2

Vonnegut's characters have been described as flat. Accepting the hypothesis that this is an authorial decision designed to emphasize the ideas of the text, delineate the symbolic roles of three of the lesser characters of *Slaughterhouse-Five*.

Outline

I.   Thesis Statement: *Valencia Pilgrim, Edgar Derby, and Bertram Rumfoord each serve primarily symbolic roles within* Slaughterhouse-Five.

II. Valencia

    A. Obsessed with silver pattern when Billy is hospitalized

    B. Makes little attempt to understand her husband

    C. Wants party guests to admire her ring

    D. Symbol of shallowness and materialism in American culture

III. Edgar Derby

    A. Pulls strings to get into army

    B. Unfailingly kind to everyone

    C. Stands up to Campbell

    D. Gets shot for petty theft

    E. Symbol of good, but mistakenly based patriotism and injustice of war

IV. Bertram Rumfoord

    A. Thinks weak people should be killed

    B. Wants to ignore evidence contrary to his beliefs

    C. Thinks Dresden had to be bombed

    D. Symbol of myopic morality of war enthusiasts

Topic #3

Billy's Tralfamadorian adventures can be interpreted as real or imaginary. What evidence supports each view? What differing messages does each interpretation give the work as a whole?

Outline

I. Thesis Statement: *While it is difficult to decide whether Billy's outer-space adventures are real or imaginary, each interpretation sheds an interesting light on the proper interpretation of the meaning of* Slaughterhouse-Five.

II. Billy's adventures are imaginary

    A. Repetition of "he says"

    B. Evidence of severe psychological strain

    C. Head trauma leads to proselytizing

    D. Novel is against fatalism

III. Billy's adventures are real

    A. First adventure occurs before head trauma

    B. Novel distinguishes between memories, hallucinations, and "time travel"

    C. Tralfamadorians have appeared in earlier works, thence are as real as Trout and Rosewater

    D. Billy knows when he is going to die

    E. Novel advises new philosophy: focus on the good moments in life.

SECTION ELEVEN

Bibliography

Allen, William Rodney. *Understanding Kurt Vonnegut*. South Carolina: University of South Carolina, 1991.

Broer, Lawrence R. *Sanity Plea: Schizophrenia in the Novels of Kurt Vonnegut*. Tuscaloosa: University of Alabama Press, 1994 (1989).

Klinkowitz, Jerome, and John Somer, eds. *The Vonnegut Statement*. New York: Delacorte/Lawrence, 1973.

Klinkowitz, Jerome. *Kurt Vonnegut*. New York: Methuen, 1982.

Loeb, Monica. *Vonnegut's Duty-Dance with Death: Theme and Structure in* Slaughterhouse-Five. Sweden: Umea Universitetsbibliotek, 1979.

Lundquist, James. *Kurt Vonnegut*. New York: Ungar, 1976.

Merrill, Robert, ed. *Critical Essays on Kurt Vonnegut*. Boston: G.K. Hall, 1989.

Mustazza, Leonard, ed. *The Critical Response to Kurt Vonnegut*. Westport: Greenwood Press, 1994.

Schatt, Stanley. *Kurt Vonnegut, Jr.* Boston: Twayne, 1976.

Vonnegut, Kurt. *Slaughterhouse-Five*. New York: Delacorte Press/Seymour Lawrence, 1969.

MAXnotes®

REA's Literature Study Guides

MAXnotes® are student-friendly. They offer a fresh look at masterpieces of literature, presented in a lively and interesting fashion. **MAXnotes®** offer the essentials of what you should know about the work, including outlines, explanations and discussions of the plot, character lists, analyses, and historical context. **MAXnotes®** are designed to help you think independently about literary works by raising various issues and thought-provoking ideas and questions. Written by literary experts who currently teach the subject, **MAXnotes®** enhance your understanding and enjoyment of the work.

Available **MAXnotes®** include the following:

Absalom, Absalom!
The Aeneid of Virgil
Animal Farm
Antony and Cleopatra
As I Lay Dying
As You Like It
The Autobiography of
    Malcolm X
The Awakening
Beloved
Beowulf
Billy Budd
The Bluest Eye, A Novel
Brave New World
The Canterbury Tales
The Catcher in the Rye
The Color Purple
The Crucible
Death in Venice
Death of a Salesman
The Divine Comedy I: Inferno
Dubliners
Emma
Euripides' Medea & Electra
Frankenstein
Gone with the Wind
The Grapes of Wrath
Great Expectations
The Great Gatsby
Gulliver's Travels
Hamlet
Hard Times

Heart of Darkness
Henry IV, Part I
Henry V
The House on Mango Street
Huckleberry Finn
I Know Why the Caged
    Bird Sings
The Iliad
Invisible Man
Jane Eyre
Jazz
The Joy Luck Club
Jude the Obscure
Julius Caesar
King Lear
Les Misérables
Lord of the Flies
Macbeth
The Merchant of Venice
The Metamorphoses of Ovid
The Metamorphosis
Middlemarch
A Midsummer Night's Dream
Moby-Dick
Moll Flanders
Mrs. Dalloway
Much Ado About Nothing
My Antonia
Native Son
1984
The Odyssey
Oedipus Trilogy

Of Mice and Men
On the Road
Othello
Paradise Lost
A Passage to India
Plato's Republic
Portrait of a Lady
A Portrait of the Artist
    as a Young Man
Pride and Prejudice
A Raisin in the Sun
Richard II
Romeo and Juliet
The Scarlet Letter
Sir Gawain and the
    Green Knight
Slaughterhouse-Five
Song of Solomon
The Sound and the Fury
The Stranger
The Sun Also Rises
A Tale of Two Cities
The Taming of the Shrew
The Tempest
Tess of the D'Urbervilles
Their Eyes Were Watching God
To Kill a Mockingbird
To the Lighthouse
Twelfth Night
Uncle Tom's Cabin
Waiting for Godot
Wuthering Heights

RESEARCH & EDUCATION ASSOCIATION
61 Ethel Road W. • Piscataway, New Jersey 08854
Phone: (908) 819-8880

Please send me more information about MAXnotes®.

Name _____

Address _____

City _____ State _____ Zip _____